KB053908

WORLD
KNOWLEDGE
FORUM

NOMIC
RUM
ECONOM
FORUM
H.S. Cho

OF GIANTS
Tamir Pardo

Price
매일경제

Donald Johnston
Shin, Je-Yoon

Seoul, Korea
Steve Wozniak

WORLD
KNOWLEDGE
FORUM

MESSAGE FROM THE CHAIRMAN

As Francis Bacon, a 16th-century English philosopher, said, 'Knowledge is power'. Where this has never been truer. The World Knowledge Forum (WKF), which marks its 25th anniversary this year, is making history as the most prestigious knowledge-sharing platform for global speakers to ideas.

The WKF was born following the 1997 financial crisis with the hope that the coming 21st century will be an era centered on 'knowledge'. I launched the WKF in 2000 after two years of preparation with the aim of transforming the Republic of Korea into a knowledge driven nation.

The WKF has been leading the way in sharing knowledge by inviting world-class scholars and experts to seek solutions for the problems facing humanity and to share the results with our society. A total of more than 5,800 global speakers and 62,800 audiences have participated since the first forum was held under the theme of 'Shaping the New Millennium with Knowledge' in 2000.

This book is the WKF's history. Achievements of the WKF would not have been possible without your support and encouragement. We kindly ask for your continued anticipation of the WKF so we can repay you with richer and deeper knowledge.

Founder of the World Knowledge Forum

Chairman of Maekyung Media Group

CHANG Dae-Whan Ph.D.

Daewhan Chang

CONTENTS

WORLD
KNOWLEDGE
FORUM

2000

The 1st World Knowledge Forum

Date: October 17-19, 2000
Venue: Marriott Hotel
Theme: Shaping the New Millennium with Knowledge

Oct. 17~19, 2000
Seoul

2000

Shaping the New Millennium with Knowledge

The first World Knowledge Forum in 2000 had over 1,100 participants from 22 countries and was co-hosted by renowned global media outlets. It garnered substantial recognition as a platform for knowledge sharing. Notable speakers included Donald Johnston, Secretary-General of the OECD, Lester Thurow, MIT Professor and Heinrich Rohrer, Nobel Laureate in Physics.

Chang Dae-whan, Chairman of Maekyung Media Group, delivers the opening speech.

1

2

1. Donald Johnston, Lester Thurow, and Paul Romer (from the second left)
2. Session Participants
3. Congratulatory Message from the 15th President of South Korea, Kim Dae-jung
4. Finale of the Kim Fashion Show

2001

The 2nd World Knowledge Forum

Date: October 17-19, 2001
Venue: Marriott Hotel
Theme: Drawing the Roadmap for Knowledge Economy and Global Prosperity

2001

Drawing the Roadmap for Knowledge Economy and Global Prosperity

In an era where it was becoming increasingly important for nations and organizations to be capable of 'knowledge use', the forum aimed to develop critical knowledge for global prosperity. Over the course of three days, attendees explored changing perceptions in a knowledge-based society as well as the financial and technological challenges of the new economy.

Bill Gates, Chairman of Microsoft,
gives a keynote speech.

Productivity
Word, Excel, PowerPoint, Outlook, Access, Visio, Project
XML Business intelligence
Simple sharing
Document management
Workflow
Single canvas
매일경제
매일경제

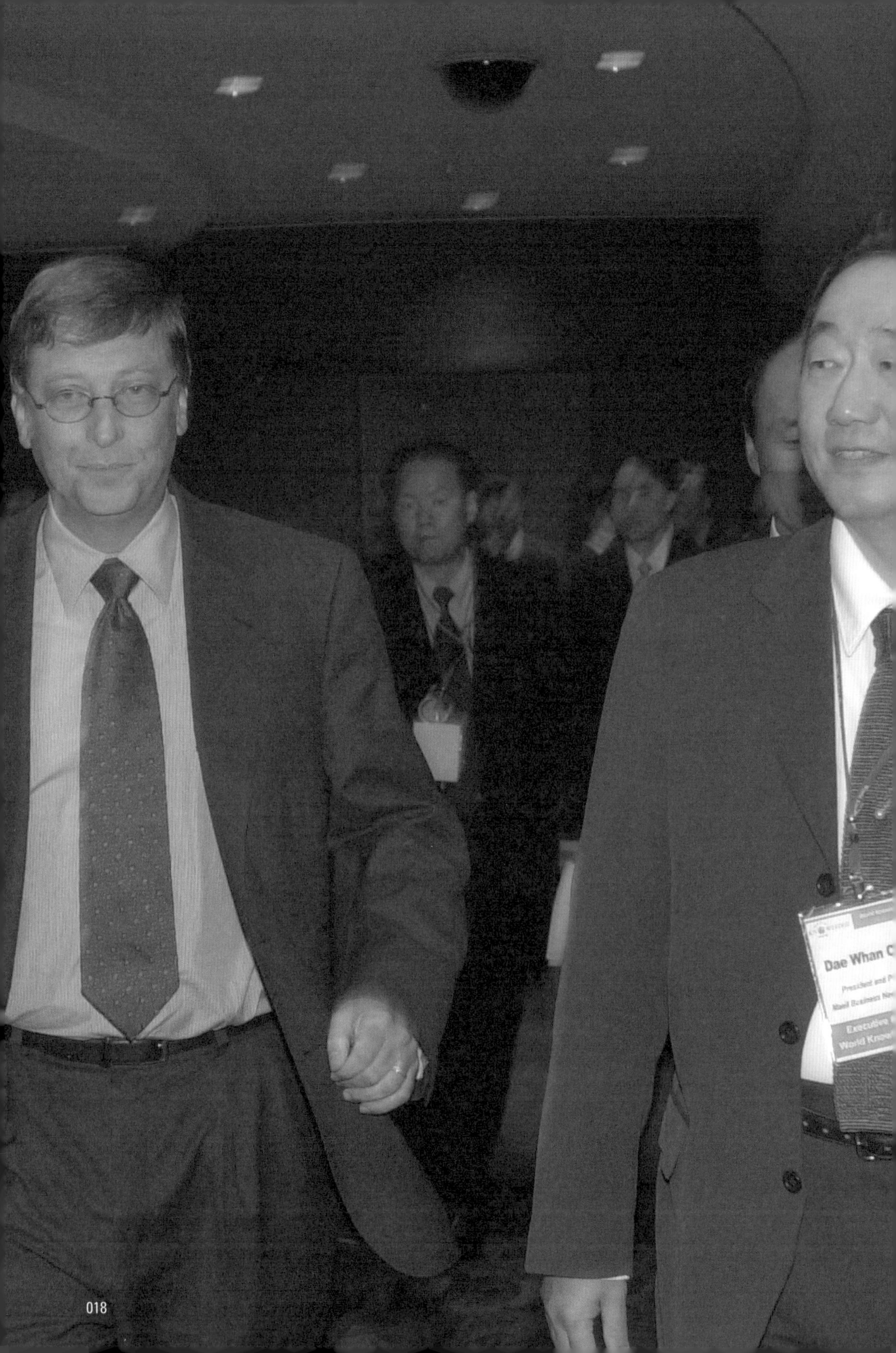
Dae Whan

Bill Gates

Chairman of Microsoft (MS), the "The Future of the Digital Decade" session

"The era of needing paper to read will soon disappear. Information devices such as tablet PCs, which will be introduced by Microsoft, will help you read long texts."

Bill Gates participated in the World Knowledge Forum (WKF) a month after the 9/11 terrorist attacks.
Though he was primarily known for delivering keynote speeches, he gave a special lecture to the audience during his session at the World Knowledge Forum.

In his brief two-day visit to Korea, Gates shared his insights on how digital technology will shape the future.
"In the future, many companies will make products related to intellectual property rights," he forecasted. "Only companies that predict how the world will change in the next 5 to 10 years and develop technologies patiently will be rewarded."

Gates anticipated that through digitizing media like books, movies and images, and by facilitating individual communication, computers will increase the productivity of knowledge workers.
As he envisioned, with the introduction of smartphones and tablet PCs, the world has undergone tremendous transformation.

2002

The 3rd World Knowledge Forum

Date: October 15-18, 2002
Venue: Sheraton Walkerhill Hotel
Theme: Knowledge in a World of Risk : A Compass towards New Prosperity

2002

Knowledge in a World of Risk: A Compass Towards New Prosperity

Analyzing transitional risks faced by individuals, companies, and nations is a crucial step in moving towards sustainable and balanced prosperity. Over 100 prominent speakers, including Philip Kotler and Stephen Covey, delivered lectures to highlight the importance of strategic adaptation in a rapidly changing world.

Applause from World Knowledge Forum session participants.

ledge Forum

1

World Knowledge Forum 2002
Special Lecture :
Oracle's e-Business Way to Win in Tough Times
Larry Ellison
Satellite
Live
Knowledge is Power!
知識=力
매일경제
MBN CNBC

2

知識
FORU

3

WORLD KNOWLEDGE FORUM
매일경
Forbes
KBS
MBN
Knowledge is
Diane Coyle
Kyung-Tae Lee
Arnoud De Meyer
Donald Johnston

1. Larry Ellison, Chairman and CEO of Oracle
2. Donald Johnston, Former Secretary-General of the OECD, and Chang Dae-whan, Chairman of Maekyung Media Group
3. OECD General Assembly
4. Joseph Stiglitz, 2001 Nobel Prize laureate in Economics, and the 15th President of South Korea, Kim Dae-jung
5. Session Participants

2003

The 4th World Knowledge Forum

Date: September 14-17, 2003
Venue: Grand Hilton Seoul Hotel
Theme: Creating a New World Order and Economy

2003

Creating a New World Order and Economy

As economic uncertainty reshaped the future, the forum discussed the creation of a new world order. Over 1,000 leaders from 50 countries gathered to examine the emerging frameworks of governments and economic systems required to foster global stability.

The 16th President of South Korea, Roh Moo-hyun, delivers a congratulatory message at the opening ceremony.

1

2

3

4

5

6

1. Jim Collins, Author of 'Good to Great'
2. Speakers of WKF (1)
3. Speakers of WKF (2)
4. The 16th President of South Korea, Roh Moo-hyun
5. Speakers of WKF (3)
6. Donald Johnston, Secretary-General of the OECD
7. Session Participants

7

2004

The 5th World Knowledge Forum

Date: October 11-13, 2004
Venue: Walkerhill Hotel & Resorts
Theme: Partnership for Renewed Growth

2004

Partnership for Renewed Growth

The forum addressed critical global challenges, ranging from the economic consequences of terrorism to China's expanding influence. Beyond offering strategies for leadership in a swiftly evolving landscape, it emphasized the vital importance of collaboration to foster resilience and drive growth.

1. External Banners of WKF
2. The 15th President of South Korea, Kim Dae-jung, delivers a congratulatory message at the opening ceremony
3. Robert Mundell, 1999 Nobel Prize laureate in Economics

1

World Knowledge Forum 2004
매일경제
MBN CNBC
WORLD KNOWLEDGE FORUM
매일경제
WORLD KNOWLEDGE FORUM
매일경제

2

dge Forum 2004
LEDGE
MBN CNBC
경제

3

WORLD
KN WLE
FORUM

Carly Fiorina

CEO of Hewlett-Packard (HP)

"Big businesses must constantly innovate in key areas that can penetrate the future."

Carly Fiorina, CEO of Hewlett Packard (HP), was one of the most sought-after at the fifth World Knowledge Forum. Fiorina left stinging advice for Korean to support them in building their core models and adapting to the new era. "All physical processes, individual contact, are digital and mobile," Fiorina said, She stressed that "In Korea, which has the most digital to mobile experience, infinite opportunities are guaranteed."

2005

The 6th World Knowledge Forum

Date: October 10-12, 2005
Venue: Walkerhill Hotel & Resorts
Theme: Creativity and Collaboration: Foundation for the New Era

2005

Creativity and Collaboration: Foundation for the New Era

The Forum addressed critical issues such as Asia's economic outlook, corporate growth drivers, and creativity. It explored challenges and business models for navigating a rapidly changing economy to establish Asia as a global economic hub and assessed the impact of Asian countries on future growth.

Paul Kennedy, Yale University professor, Lee Jae-yong, Chairman of Samsung Electronics, and Choi Tae-won, Chairman of SK, exchanging business cards.

Jay Y. Lee

wledge Forum 2005
KIEP
매일경제
mbn
매일경제TV
KIEP
mbn
매일경제TV
세계지식포럼

Jack Welch

Former chairman of GE, in keynote speech at 'The Conditions of a Successful Leader' session

"The more interested and passionate you have for your employees, the more you care about people, the more successful you are."

Jack Welch, former chairman of GE, gave a keynote speech live on satellite emphasizing the need for leaders and companies to value talent in order to achieve success.

"We should be able to reward those who take risks and be willing to make creative talents heroes," he said.

Having become the youngest GE chairman in 1981, Welch is a legendary manager who has led GE for more than 20 years and raised its corporate value from $12 billion to $450 billion.

According to Welch, GE's primary strengths are its people resources rather than its manufacturing prowess. "You can't be a great leader if you don't tell employees exactly where they are and what they can do," he stated.

"Managers themselves should be role models for employees to follow."

2006

The 7th World Knowledge Forum

Date: October 17-19, 2006
Venue: Walkerhill Hotel & Resorts
Theme: Creative Economy

2006

Creative Economy

Creative economies rely on the intellectual capital generated by skilled thinkers. The World Knowledge Forum discussed our current position and future direction in the value-creating economy, emphasizing the importance of creativity. Under the theme "Creative Economy," leading scholars and business leaders from around the world attended to explore new avenues for value creation in the 21st century.

George Soros, Chairman of Soros Fund Management, gives a special lecture.

1

2

3

1. George Soros, Chairman of Soros Fund Management
2. Opening Plenary **3.** VIP Dinner **4.** China Business Session
5. Chang Dae-hwan and George Soros **6.** Michael Porter

SK corporation
LG
HYUNDAI
SAMSUNG ELECTRONICS
posco
KB Kookmin Bank
GS E&C
WOORI BANK
KEB
Liping He
Songzuo Xiang
Zhou Chen
Gary Dirks

4

mbn
매일경제TV
매일경제
KNOWLEDGE
FORUM

5

World Knowledge Forum 2006

6

2007

The 8th World Knowledge Forum

Date: October 16-18, 2007
Venue: Walkerhill Hotel & Resorts
Theme: Wealth Creation & Asia

2007

Wealth Creation & Asia

As economic competition intensified and new challenges emerged, the prominence of Asia, with its growing economies and technological advances, reshaped the global landscape - humanity had now entered the 'Asian century'. While Asia, particularly China and India, began driving a significant portion of global growth, it also faced serious issues such as widening inequality, regional conflicts, and environmental damage. The forum explored how creative knowledge and innovation can address these challenges and turn chaotic changes into opportunities for wealth creation.

Tadashi Agi, Author of 'Drops of God', signs his book.

World Knowledge Forum 200
세계지식포럼 2007
World Knowledge Forum
Alan Greenspan
Former Chairman,
Federal Reserve Board
매일경제
mbn
1

2

3

4

1. A conversation with former Federal Reserve Board (FRB) Chairman Alan Greenspan
2. Colin Powell and Attendees
3. Former U.S. Secretary of State Colin Powell
4. Korean Actor Park Shin-yang attends the Wine Party

2008

The 9th World Knowledge Forum

Date: October 14-16, 2008
Venue: Walkerhill Hotel & Resorts
Theme: Collabonomics & Greater Asia

2008

Collabonomics & Greater Asia

The term 'Collabonomic' (Collaboration + Economics) represents the new approach to generating wealth in the 21st century through collaboration. The forum explored how cross-sector partnerships can tackle global challenges, drive innovation, and foster growth amid economic uncertainty. It highlighted the crucial role of collaboration in advancing Asian economic integration and mitigating global risks.

Richard Branson, Chairman of Virgin Group, delivers the opening speech via satellite.

'09 World Knowlec
World Knowledge Forum 2008
Collabonomics & Greater Asia
Specia
Richard Bran
& Founder o
매일경제
mbn

1. Session Participants
2. A Conversation between Chang Dae-whan and Eric Maskin
3. Michael Porter, Professor of Harvard University
4. OECD General Assembly
5. WKF Staff Members

3

Pier Carlo Padoan
Narayan Pant
WORLD KNOWLEDGE FORUM
World Knowledge Forum
Collabonomics & Greater Asia

4

2008
World Knowledge Forum

5

2009

The 10th World Knowledge Forum

Date: October 13-15, 2009
Venue: Walkerhill Hotel & Resorts
Theme: One Asia: New Economic Order & Recovery

2009

One Asia: New Economic Order & Recovery

Asia rose as a pivotal force in the international stage, driven by lessons learned from past economic crises and substantial cash reserves accumulated over time. The 10th World Knowledge Forum examined Asia's economic ascent and the need for deeper cooperation. Leaders and academics from around the world emphasized Asia's role in the global economy and sought solutions for future recovery and the creation of a new world order.

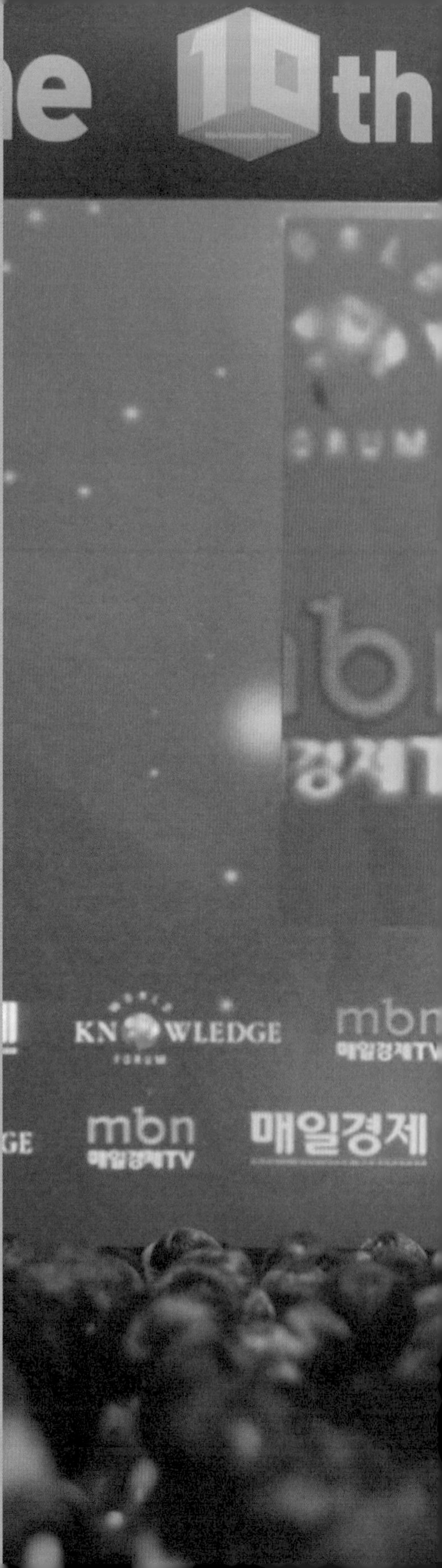

George W. Bush, the 43rd President of the United States, delivers the keynote address at the inauguration ceremony at the Sheraton Walkerhill Hotel, which is attended by more than 1,300 guests.

World Knowledge
mbn
매일경제TV
The 10th
매일경제
KN WLEDGE
FORUM
WLEDGE

1

2

1. Robert Mundell, Columbia University Professor
2. Kevan Watts, Chairman of Merrill Lynch International
3. Lee Jae-yong, Chairman of Samsung Electronics, and George W. Bush, the 43rd President of the United States
4. Fashion Show by André Kim

George W. Bush

The 43rd President of the United States, delivered the keynote speech on the 'Role of Asian countries, including South Korea, should play in the process of reorganizing the world order and the Korea-U.S. relationship'

"The future of the global economy depends on one Asia."

Former US President George W. Bush delivered a keynote speech on the 'The Role Asian countries, including South Korea, should play in the process of reorganizing world order and the Korea-U.S. relationship'. The year following the 2008 global financial crisis, the World Knowledge Forum was held under the theme of "One Asia, New Economic Order and Economic Recovery." Bush stressed that the world's economic center is moving from the Atlantic Ocean to the Pacific, and that the way for Asia to become more prosperous is to foster economic freedom, including the creation of a free trade zone. Referring to the 2008 financial crisis, he also emphasized that countries around the world must escape the temptation of protectionism, which has been growing since the crisis. Furthermore, he stated that after the global crisis, we will see how much Asia has contributed to its resolution, and that he agrees with Korea's call for the establishment of an Asia-Pacific Free Trade Zone.

2010

The 11th World Knowledge Forum

Date: October 12-14, 2010
Venue: Walkerhill Hotel & Resorts
Theme: One Asia Momentum, G20 Leadership & CreatInnovation

2010

One Asia Momentum, G20 Leadership & CreatInnovation

Historically, Asia was frequently criticized as the source of local economic crises. However, Asia's resilience and robust recovery were crucial in averting a global economic collapse triggered by the U.S. The forum highlighted Asia's increasing influence on the world stage and the vision of One Asia to promote greater economic integration and enhance cooperation among Asian countries.

Girls' Generation performs at the welcome dinner for the 11th World Knowledge Forum.

24
7
32
9
21

1

2

3

4

1. Yukio Hatoyama, the 93rd Prime Minister of Japan
2. Richard Branson, Chairman of Virgin Group
3. Session participants reading the Maeil Business Newspaper
4. Niall Ferguson, Harvard University Professor

2011

The 12th World Knowledge Forum

Date: October 11-13, 2011
Venue: Walkerhill Hotel & Resorts
Theme: The New Economic Crisis: Reforming Global Leadership & Asia's Challenge

2011

The New Economic Crisis: Reforming Global Leadership & Asia's Challenge

Despite initial expectations of economic growth at the start of the year, the global economy plunged following the U.S. default risk in July, which led to the U.S. credit rating downgrade, compounded by the eurozone's financial crisis. The forum addressed the resulting economic downturn and the urgent need for leadership reform, highlighting Asia's pivotal role in overcoming the crisis and seeking collaborative solutions with global leaders.

Michael Sandel signs books for participants.

will be given
MBN

The 12th World Knowledge Forum
매일경제

3

4

1. Lee Soo-man, Former Producer of SM Entertainment
2. 'Global CEO Roundtable' session
3. Gordon Brown, Former Prime Minister of the United Kingdom
4. Gordon Brown and Michael Sandel

2012

The 13th World Knowledge Forum

Date: October 15-17, 2012
Venue: Walkerhill Hotel & Resorts
Theme: The Great Breakthrough: New Solutions for Global Crisis

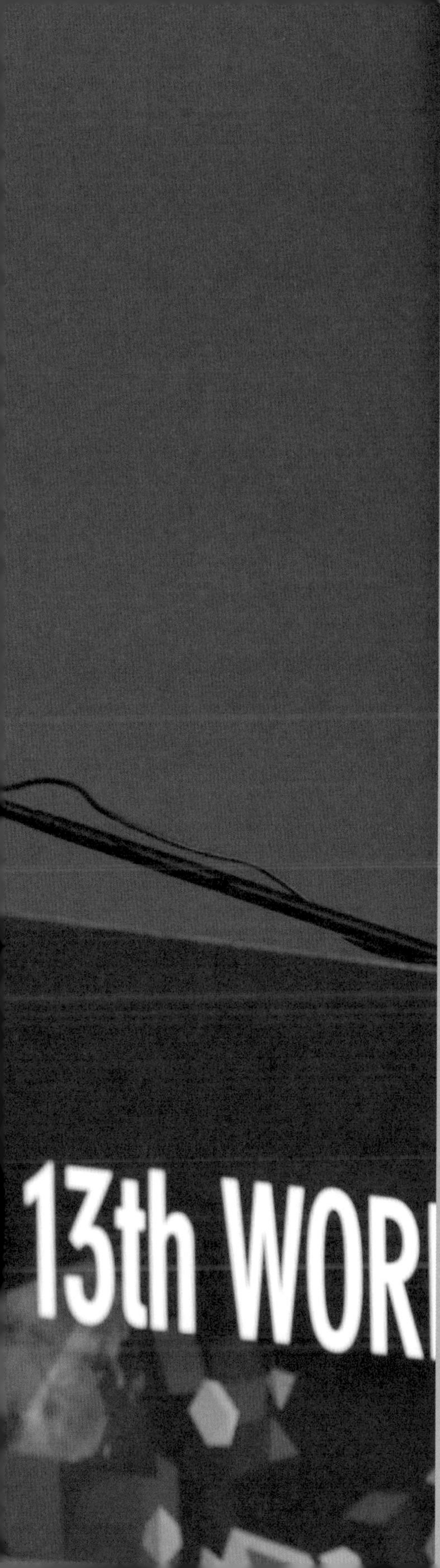

2012

The Great Breakthrough: New Solutions for Global Crisis

Fueled by new perspectives, emerging countries reshaped global economic governance. Ultimately, nations that embraced innovative economic solutions and creative leadership thrived in the evolving global landscape. This creative leadership was crucial not only for national leaders but also for business executives. The forum explored ways to address changes in the global economy through the lenses of leadership, ethics, creativity, and happiness.

The 18th President of South Korea, Park Geun-hye, delivers a congratulatory speech at the opening ceremony.

1

2

1. Malcolm Gladwell, Journalist at The New Yorker
2. Paul Krugman, City University of New York professor
3. Gala Dinner
4. Condoleezza Rice, The 66th United States Secretary of State

2013

The 14th World Knowledge Forum

Date: October 15-17, 2013
Venue: Walkerhill Hotel & Resorts
Theme: The One Asia Metamorphosis

2013

The One Asia Metamorphosis

Having gone through the European financial crisis that immediately followed the broader global financial crisis, the world economy experienced a vast, unprecedented shift. Emerging nations also started raising their voices, changing the world's power structures. In 2013, the forum re-illuminated Asian values as a starting point for addressing the limits of the current capitalist system. It highlighted the need for innovative thinking to overcome current challenges and Asia's important role in resolving global crises.

Gregory Mankiw, Professor of Harvard University, greets a his fan.

맨큐의경제학
MAEKYUNG MEDIA GROUP
WORLD KNOWLEDGE FORUM

1

2

3

4

5

1. A conversation with Richard Florida
2. Daphne Koller, Co-founder of Coursera
3. Hermann Simon, Chairman of Simon-Kucher & Partners
4. Session Hall
5. Speaker of WKF
6. Richard Florida, Professor

6

2014

The 15th World Knowledge Forum

Date: October 14-16, 2014
Venue: The Shilla Seoul
Theme: Invigorating the Global Economy

2014

Invigorating the Global Economy

Even after emerging from the protracted global financial crisis, the international economy remained hampered by slow growth. Meanwhile, technological innovations, represented by robotics and the Internet of Things (IoT), portended a significant shift to a new digital era and offered opportunities to spur the flagging global economy. The forum's main topics were risk considerations that different nations face and how technology advancements might be leveraged to lessen such risks.

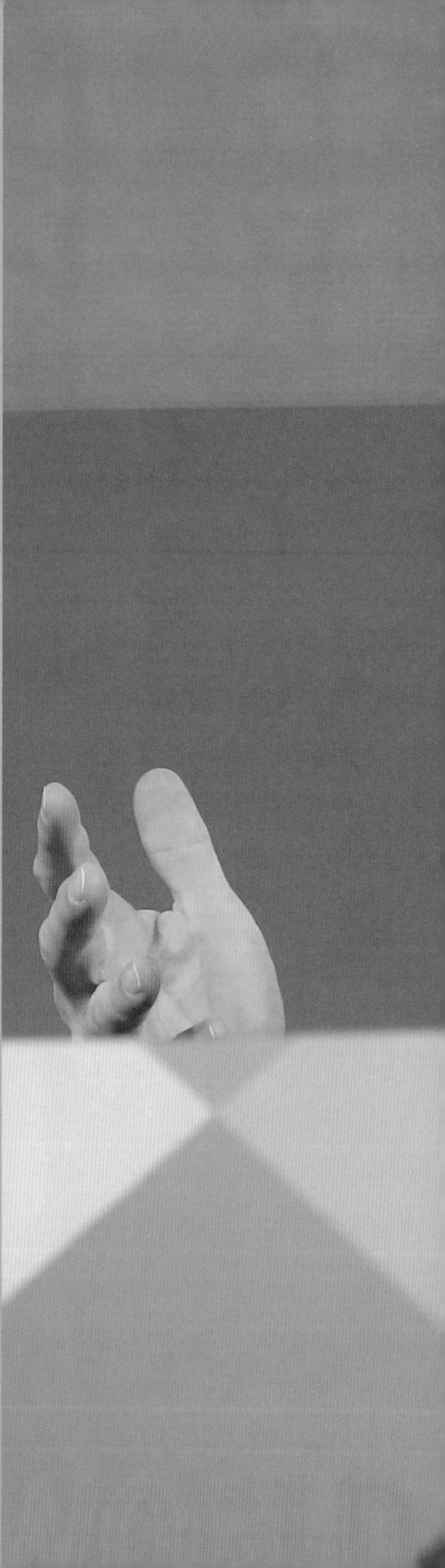

Nicolas Sarkozy, the 23rd President of France, gives a speech at the opening ceremony of the 15th World Knowledge Forum.

15th

Gino Yu
Hong Kong Polytechnic University School of Design
The 15th
WORLD KNOWLEDGE FORUM
1

Speaker
Thomas Piketty
The 15th
WORLD
KNOWLEDGE
FORUM
매일경제 MBN
2

매일경제
The 15th
WORLD KNOWLEDGE FORUM
3

1. 'Consumer Robot' session
2. A conversation with Thomas Piketty
3. Staff Members
4. Book signing by Andrew McAfee
5. Opening Ceremony

2015

The 16th World Knowledge Forum

Date: October 20-22, 2015
Venue: Jangchung Arena·The Shilla Seoul
Theme: Mapping the Zeitgeist

2015

Mapping the Zeitgeist

In order to survive in a world where global paradigms were constantly shifting, we had to discover a fresh modern zeitgeist. The forum explored strategic responses for individuals, companies, and nations in the era of the "sharing economy." The forum also featured sessions on emerging growth drivers, including wearables, robotics, IoT, and fintech.

Fumitake Koga and Ichiro Kishimi, the authors of 'The Courage to Be Disliked' engage in conversation with MBN anchor Kim Joo-ha.

Mapping
the ZEITGEIST
Mapping
the ZEITGEIST
매일경제 MBN

1

2

3

1. Key speakers of the 16th World Knowledge Forum
2. 'The Courage to Be Disliked' session
3. 'Global Economy from Dr. Doom' session by Nouriel Roubini
4. Book signing event by Don Tapscott
5. Session Hall

4

5
THE 16TH
WORLD KNOWLEDGE FORUM
Mapping the ZEITGEIST
Leon Panetta
Na Kyung-Won
Yoichi Masuzoe
Han Min Koo

Ichiro Kishimi & Fumitake Koga

Author of "Courage to be Disliked" during the "Courage to be Disliked" session

"Happiness can be gained when you accept yourself as you are, are prepared to be hated by others, and have the courage to enter people."

Ichiro Kishimi and Fumitake Koga, the writers of "Courage to be Disliked," convened at Jangchung Arena ahead of a sizable crowd. The popularity of the two authors was evident from the attendance of almost 3,500 individuals at the event. Kishimi advised, "All concerns come from interpersonal relationships. Nevertheless, to feel happy, you have to go into interpersonal relationships. That's why you have to have the courage to be disliked." Kishimi is a Western philosophy expert who studied Plato and discovered Adler psychology while raising a child. Adler is a psychologist who contends that individuals have the power to alter their destiny by their decisions. Adler is a psychologist who argues that people can change their future depending on their choice.

Adler adds that "Even if nothing materializes, this moment is everything in your life, so don't waste your life waiting for something to come true".

2016

The 17th World Knowledge Forum

Date: October 11-13, 2016
Venue: Jangchung Arena·The Shilla Seoul
Theme: Aiming for Great Instauration

2016

Aiming for Great Instauration

The forum sought ways to fundamentally change the world by sharing science-based knowledge and the restoration of new leadership. Top experts in various fields across politics, economics, science, and technology gathered to explore new directions for the world, aiming to engage a broad audience in this transformative effort.

Gerhard Schröder, the 7th Chancellor of Germany, gives a speech in the session 'Brexit and the Future of Europe'.

1

2

3

THE 17th WORLD KNOWLEDGE FORUM
Aiming for GREAT INSTAURATION
Wendy Sherman
Kim Chong In
David Rubenstein
4

5

6

1. 'The Future Changed by Drones' session
2. Dick Cheney
3. Wendy Sherman
4. Speakers and Participants
5. The 17th World Knowledge Forum Banner
6. Ban Ki-moon, the 8th Secretary-General of the United Nations

2017

The 18th World Knowledge Forum

Date: October 17-19, 2017
Venue: Jangchung Arena·The Shilla Seoul
Theme: Inflection Point: Towards New Prosperity

2017

Inflection Point: Towards New Prosperity

The history of humankind has met several inflection points. In 2017, we face another inflection point - the so-called Fourth Industrial Revolution, driven by the technological innovation and advancement of AI. The 18th World Knowledge Forum was organized to explore ways for the world to respond more wisely at this critical juncture. It featured discussions on managing these changes, with a key focus on the widely recognized concept of the Fourth Industrial Revolution.

David Hanson provides a demonstration of a humanoid robot in the 'Humanizing Robots' session.

18th
Arena

1

1. Hillary Clinton, the 67th U.S. Secretary of State, with Chang Dae-whan, Chairman of Maekyung Media Group

2. Jangchung Arena
3. Foreign Filming Team
4. Bruce Bennett

제18회 세계지식포럼
THE 18th WORLD KNOWLEDGE FORUM
Inflection Point :
Towards New Prosperity
변곡점을 넘어 새로운 번영을 향해
매일경제 MBN
MBN
정문
THE 18th WORLD KNOWLEDGE FORUM
2

매일경제
3

4

2018

The 19th World Knowledge Forum

Date: October 10-12, 2018
Venue: Jangchung Arena·The Shilla Seoul
Theme: Collective Intelligence: Overcoming Global Pandemonium

2018

Collective Intelligence: Overcoming Global Pandemonium

John Milton refers to "Pandemonium" as the devil's den in his poem "Paradise Lost." Essentially, the term is used to depict situations of chaos and confusion. In 2018, global challenges such as geopolitical conflicts and trade wars brought society into a collective state of pandemonium. To overcome these hurdles, the forum discussed creating trust-based ecosystems through blockchain technology to enhance the competitiveness of nations and companies.

Janet Yellen, the 78th U.S. Secretary of the Treasury, smiles at the participants while speaking in the session 'Global Economic Outlook by Janet Yellen'.

1

AMERICAN
AND THE FATE OF
THE 19th WORLD KNOWLEDGE FORUM
OVERCOMING
COLLECTIVE INTELLIGENCE
CHAOS
THAT REMINDS ME OF GREECE AND SPARTA!
NATIONALISM
WAR
MIGRATION
CHANG DAE-WHAN
FINANCIAL CRISIS
THE FIRST ROUGH DRAFT OF HISTORY
WHAT WE NEED IS
TIKI TAKA
매일경제
MBN
BAN
MINDS
GLOBAL PROBLEMS REQUIRE GLOBAL SOLUTIONS
CLIMATE CHANGE IS HAPPENING!

2

THE 19th
WORLD KNOWLEDGE FORUM

1. Drawing performance during the 'Upgrading Manufacturing & Successful Strategy for Smart Factory' session
2. Kersti Kaljulaid, The 5th President of Estonia
3. Vice Chairman of Maekyung Media Group, Jang Chang Seung-joon, with Kersti Kaljulaid, the 5th President of Estonia
4. Sculptures at the Event Venue

2019

The 20th World Knowledge Forum

Date: September 25-27, 2019
Venue: Jangchung Arena·The Shilla Seoul
Theme: Knowledge Revolution 5.0:
Perspicacity Towards Prosperity for All

2019

Knowledge Revolution 5.0: Perspicacity Towards Prosperity for All

After four explosive knowledge revolutions, humanity reached the midst of Knowledge Revolution 5.0 in 2019. The Knowledge Revolution 5.0 refers to an entirely new approach in which society can advance when accompanied by proper technological development. The forum set the stage for candid discussions to cultivate perspicacity that could unlock a new world for humankind.

Richard Browning, CEO of Gravity Industries, demonstrates a jet suit.

WORLD

1

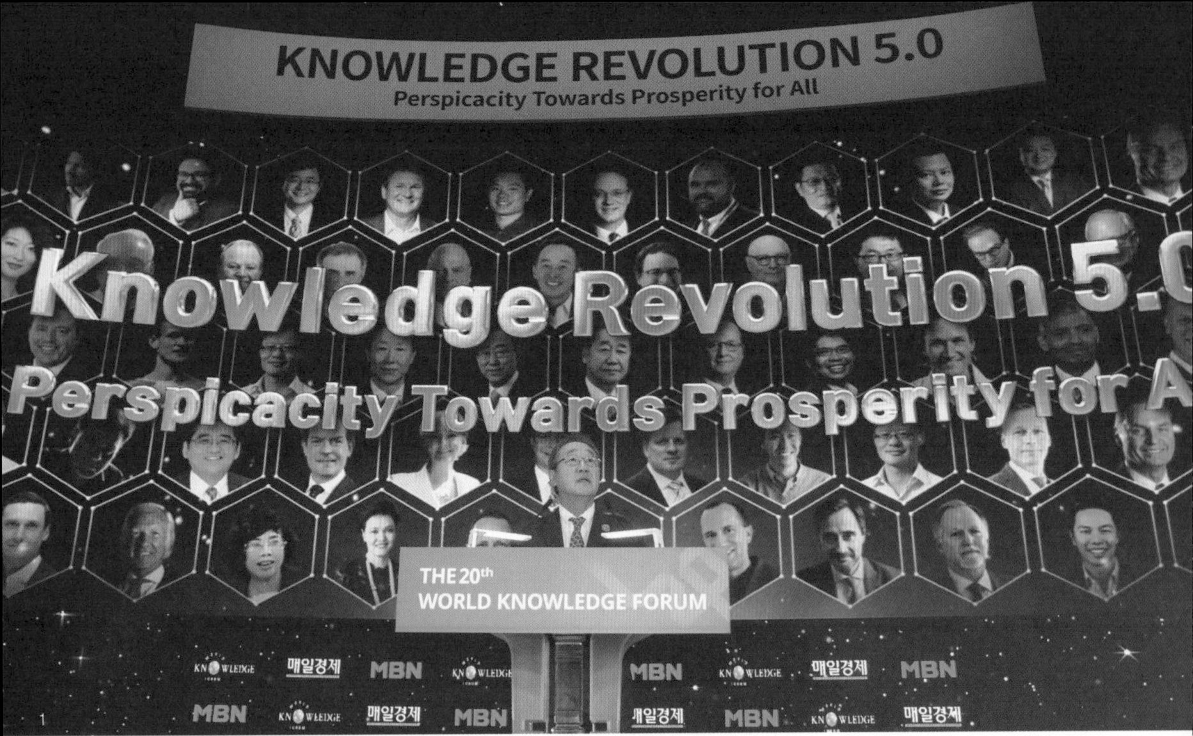

2

1. Chang Dae-whan, Chairman of Maekyung Media Group
2. YouTube stars of the 'mukbang' community
3. Professor Niall Ferguson
4. Jo Malone, Founder of Jo Loves
5. Moon Jae-in, The 19th President of South Korea,
6. Opening ceremony celebration show

3

4

KNOWLEDGE REVOLUTION 5.0
WORLD KNOWLEDGE FORUM
WORLD KNOWLEDGE FORUM
20th WKF
5

6

THE 20th WORLD KNOWLEDGE FORUM
Knowledge Revolution 5.0

2020

The 21st World Knowledge Forum

Date: September 16-18, 2020
Venue: The Shilla Seoul
Theme: Pandenomics Perspective:
Shaping New Global Symbiosis

2020

Pandenomics Perspective: Shaping New Global Symbiosis

Pandenomics, a combination of the words 'pandemic' and 'economics', signifies a new survival paradigm aimed at overcoming the pandemic crisis and achieving shared prosperity through global cooperation. In less than a year after the COVID-19 outbreak, the death toll has topped half a million, and a global recession has begun. The 21st World Knowledge Forum aimed to navigate the sudden disorder brought by the pandemic.

Theresa May, the 76th Prime Minister of the United Kingdom, attends the opening ceremony of the 21st World Knowledge Forum.

H.S. Cho
매일경제
KNOWLEDGE
1

2

Theresa May
3

PAN
DEN
MIC
O
S
MBN
SEOUL·U
매경미디어그룹
MAEKYUNG MEDIA GROUP
SEOULSTARTUP
4

5

6

1. Klaus Schwab, Chairman of the World Economic Forum
2. Seo Jung-jin, Chairman of Celltrion
3. Theresa May, The 76th Prime Minister of the United Kingdom
4. 'Untact Discussion' in the Pandemic Era
5. Participants watching a session via zoom
6. Sanitizing gate at the Entrance
7. Session Hall

7

2021

The 22nd World Knowledge Forum

Date: September 14-16, 2021
Venue: Jangchung Arena·The Shilla Seoul
Theme: Terraincognita: Redesigning the Global Architecture

2021

Terra Incognita: Redesigning the Global Architecture

The forum examined post-pandemic potential, the new zeitgeist, and the balance of powers. The halting of global activities caused by the pandemic served as a reminder of the necessity of interdependence. At this pivotal moment in history, thought leaders convened to contemplate how to move forward in the spirit of coexistence.

Kim Yeon-koung, former South Korean national volleyball player, Discusses the theme 'From Tokyo to Beijing, and Then Seoul' with the IOC Chairman.

1. Marc Raibert introducing Spot
2. Choi Si-won, Member of Super Junior
3. 'Justice in Our Time' session with Michael Sandel
4. Lee Jae-myung, Member of Parliament, and Mike Pompeo, the 70th U.S. Secretary of State

GLOBA ARCH
WORLD KNOWLEDGE FORUM
Young Gil Song
매일경제 MBN
WORLD KNOWLEDGE FORUM
Jun-seok Lee
NING THE GLOB
3

4

WORLD KNOWLEDGE FORUM
Jae-Myung LEE
STAFF

LD KNOWLEDGE FORUM 202
mitwijumeoni
2시간 전
TOKYO 20
8분 전
bosomi0816
1시간 전
WORLD
KNOWLEDGE
FORUM

Kim Yeon-koung

Korean volleyball player during 'Tokyo to Beijing, and Seoul' session

"I desperately looked for a way to succeed as a player because on standby when I was in middle school, and I agonized over becoming a player necessary for the game. I was able to rise to where I am now because of these days."

The 22nd World Knowledge Forum was held a month after the closing of the Tokyo Olympics. Captain Kim Yeon-koung, who led the Korean women's volleyball team to the semifinals, gave a speech in a nervous voice. In the midst of the COVID-19 pandemic, the World Knowledge Forum was held in a hybrid form with a combined online and in-person audience. Kim's session was also released on various platforms such as YouTube and Zoom. Kim is known to have risen to her current position through ceaseless efforts from when she was in middle school. "I didn't wait for the opportunity to come sitting on the bench," she said. "I think I became a player who reads the game better than anyone else because I constantly analyzed and played mental simulations while watching the game." Kim added, "What young people want the most these days is fairness and justice, and sportsmanship that fights fairly toward its goals and accepts the results is fairness and justice."

2022

The 23rd World Knowledge Forum

Date: September 20-22, 2022
Venue: Jangchung Arena·The Shilla Seoul
Theme: Supercompensation: Restoring Global Prosperity & Freedom

2022

Supercompensation: Restoring Global Prosperity & Freedom

The global community stood at a turning point, with Russia's invasion of Ukraine reshaping the international order and sparking a new era of geopolitical and economic division. The forum sought out solutions that will go beyond recovering from current challenges, aiming to build a safer future in which humanity's values are protected.

Min-jin Lee, best-selling author, delivers a speech on the theme 'Pachinko and the Korean Sentiment.'

SATION:

WORLD
KNOWLEDGE
FORUM
2022
매일경제 MBN

1

SPEAKER

2

3

Chang, Seungjoon
장승준
Vice Chairman
MAEKYUNG MEDIA GROUP

4

5

6

1. Session Hall
2. 'Conversation with Tony Fernandes' session
3. Oat Drink Showcase
4. Kam Ghaffarian, Founder and Chairman of Axiom Space, and Chang Seungjoon, Vice Chairman of the Maekyung Media Group
5. Princess Haifa Al Saud of Saudi Vice Minister of Tourism
6. Jiboongi, Official Mascot of WKF
7. Oh Se-hoon, Mayor of Seoul

7

Min-jin Lee

Min-jin Lee, author of the novel 'Pachinko' during her session on 'Pachinko and Korean Sentiment'

"I thought the novel's theme could make many people uncomfortable. However, there were people whose young children read it and talked with their parents and grandparents, who experienced difficult times. The book became a medium and gave them a chance to heal their trauma."

Min-jin Lee, the author of Pachinko, a novel telling the story of Koreans in Japan for a century, from Yeongdo, Busan, to Japan. shared her perspective on the power of writing at the World Knowledge Forum. Her novel was dramatized on Apple TV and became a big hit. Lee said, "When I was in middle school, I wrote a letter to the government office on behalf of my father and got them to remove a tree that was about to fall in front of my house," adding, "I learned a great lesson that writing can change something, and I think the artist is a person who can exert influence that changes the world." Lee also offered words of support to readers who dream of becoming writers. "I tell my students to be experts in communication, not to be writers," she said. "I advise you to be honest with yourself. Don't try to be someone else. I advise you to be braver and bolder."

2023

The 24th World Knowledge Forum

Date: September 12-14, 2023
Venue: Jangchung Arena·The Shilla Seoul
Theme: Techno Big Bang: Humanity on the Shoulders of Giants

2023

Techno Big Bang: Humanity on the Shoulders of Giants

Advances in AI, quantum computing, biotechnology, and robotics are not only improving our lives, but also creating new industries and driving human prosperity. In a time when precious values like freedom and democracy are being shaken by conflicts and divisions among major powers, the forum examined whether these technological innovations could open the door to a new utopia.

Steve Wozniak, Co-founder of Apple, delivers the keynote speech at the opening ceremony of the World Knowledge Forum.

MAEKYUNG MEDIA GROUP
Steve Wozniak

1

WORLD KNOWLEDGE FORUM
WORLD KNOWLEDGE FORUM

2

WORLD KNOWLEDGE FORUM
WORLD KNOWLEDGE FORUM
WORLD KNOWLEDGE FORUM

3

WORLD KNOWLEDGE FORUM
테크노빅뱅 :
WORLD KNOWLEDGE FORUM
TECHNO BIG BANG:
HUMANITY ON THE SHOULDERS OF GIANTS
매일경제
MBN

4

5

1. Gala Dinner with Opera Singer Jo Su-mi
2. 'FRIDA: Promoting Human Creativity Using Robotics' Session
3. Anthony Fauci, The 5th Director of the U.S. National Institute of Allergy and Infectious Diseases
4. Ben Nelson and Sam Altman
5. Night Celebrating the 100th Anniversary of the Founding of Turkey
6. 'Techno bigbang and Global Economic Challenges' Session

6

FORUM
September 12 - 14, 2023
Seoul, Korea
WORLD KNOWLEDGE FORUM
MAEKYUNG MEDIA GROUP
Founder of Apple Computer, Inc.

Steve Wozniak

Co-Founder of Apple, During 'A Conversations with Steve Wozniak' Session

"Everyone is focusing on AI, but controling speed is necessary. The error of AI is still clear. A (Artificial) of AI can be replaced, but only humans can do I (Intelligence)."

Steve Wozniak, Apple co-founder and a maestro of digital invention, warned against "unconditional blind faith in Al" during a keynote lecture at the World Knowledge Forum. He stressed that "Generation Al has many hallucinations and requires a human editor." Furthermore, Wozniak stated, "Just because artificial intelligence is abused does not imply that artificial intelligence is harmful. It is bad news for those who utilize it for evil."

Just because technology has side effects does not mean you should be terrified of it. When asked if a balance between innovation and regulation is conceivable, Wozniak responded, "Effective regulation is impossible," adding, "We cannot predict and regulate all the changes that technology will bring, just as we did not think spam mail would appear when we designed the Internet."

WORLD
KNOWLEDGE
FORUM

25 Years of the World Knowledge Forum

초판 1쇄 2024년 09월 10일

엮은이 매일경제 지식부
사진 매일경제 사진부
펴낸이 허연
편집장 유승현
편집부 서정욱 정혜재 김민보 장아름 이예슬
마케팅 김성현 한동우 구민지
경영지원 김민화 오나리
디자인 김보현

펴낸곳 매경출판㈜
등록 2003년 4월 24일(No. 2-3759)
주소 (04557) 서울시 중구 충무로 2 (필동1가) 매일경제 별관 2층 매경출판㈜
홈페이지 www.mkpublish.com **스마트스토어** smartstore.naver.com/mkpublish
페이스북 @maekyungpublishing **인스타그램** @mkpublishing
전화 02)2000-2630(기획편집) 02)2000-2646(마케팅) 02)2000-2606(구입 문의)
팩스 02)2000-2609 **이메일** publish@mkpublish.co.kr
인쇄 · 제본 ㈜M-print 031)8071-0961
ISBN 979-11-6484-711-2(03320)

책값은 뒤표지에 있습니다.
파본은 구입하신 서점에서 교환해 드립니다.